Sautillé Studies

for the cello

Book One

by Cassia Harvey

CHP163

©2006 by C. Harvey Publications All Rights Reserved.

www.charveypublications.com - print books
www.learnstrings.com - PDF downloadable books
www.harveystringarrangements.com - chamber music

Sautille Studies for the Cello

Book One

Cassia Harvey

I

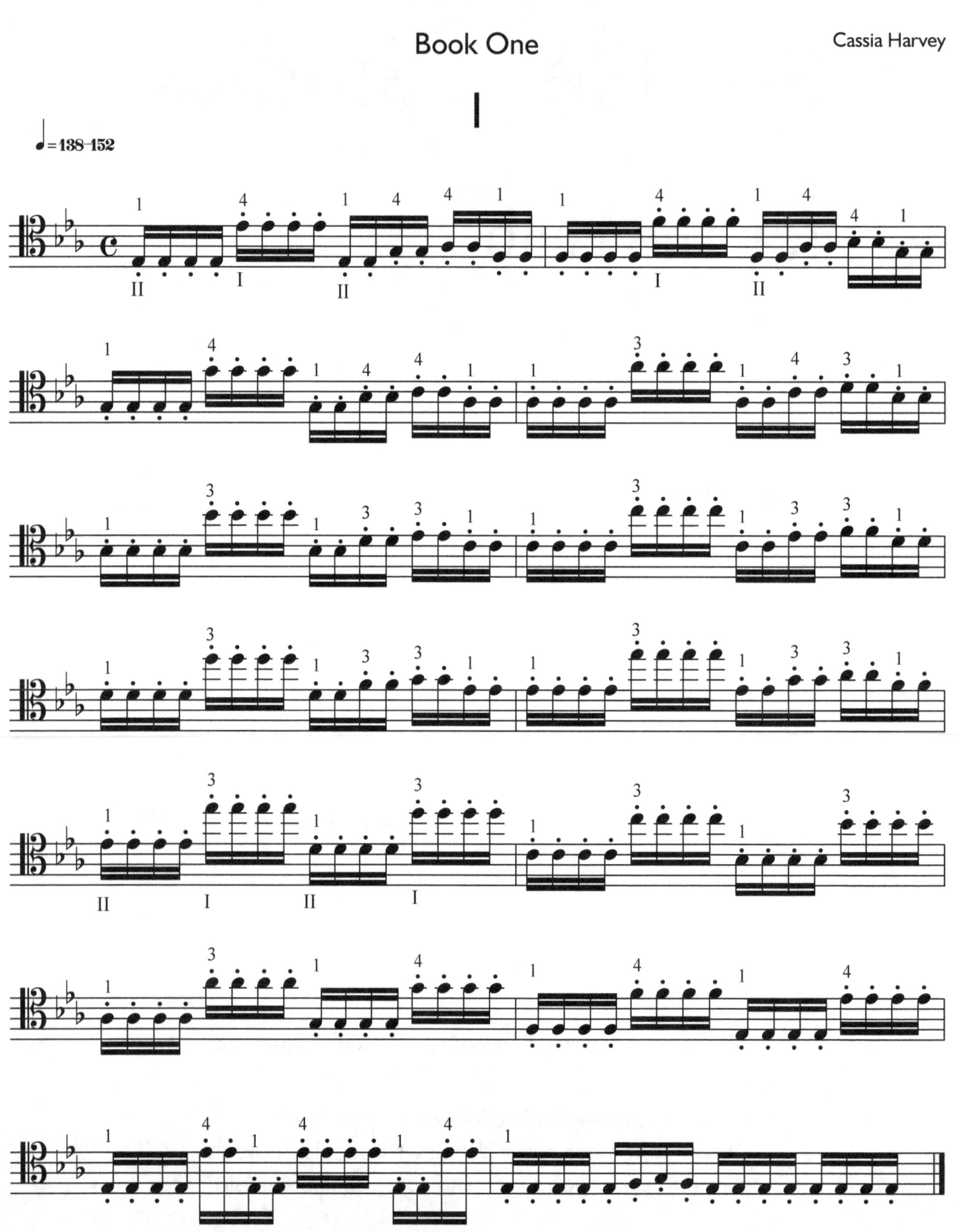

©2006 C. Harvey Publications All Rights Reserved.

Sautille Studies for the Cello, Book One

2

3

This entire page is played on the D string.

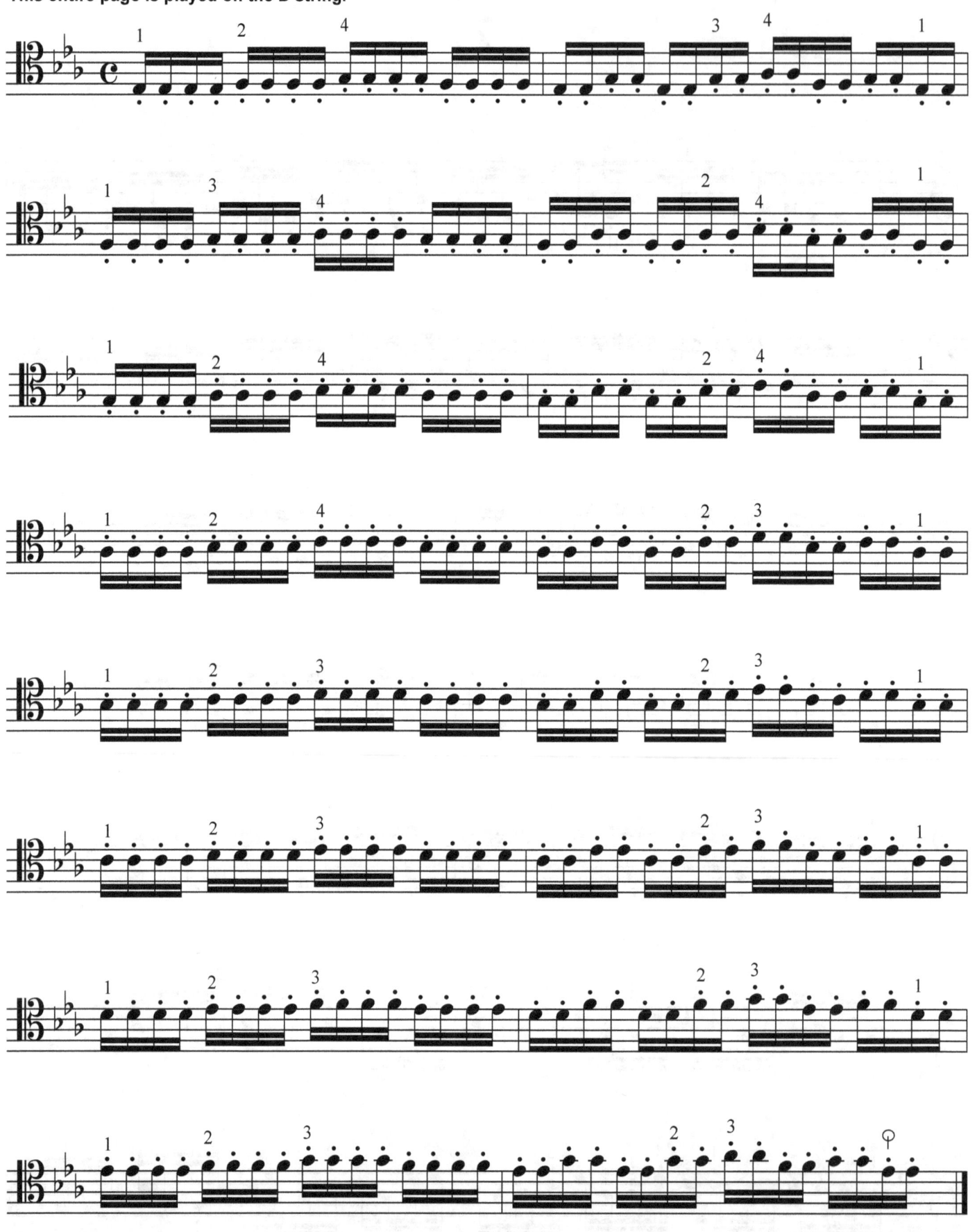

Sautille Studies for the Cello, Book One

4

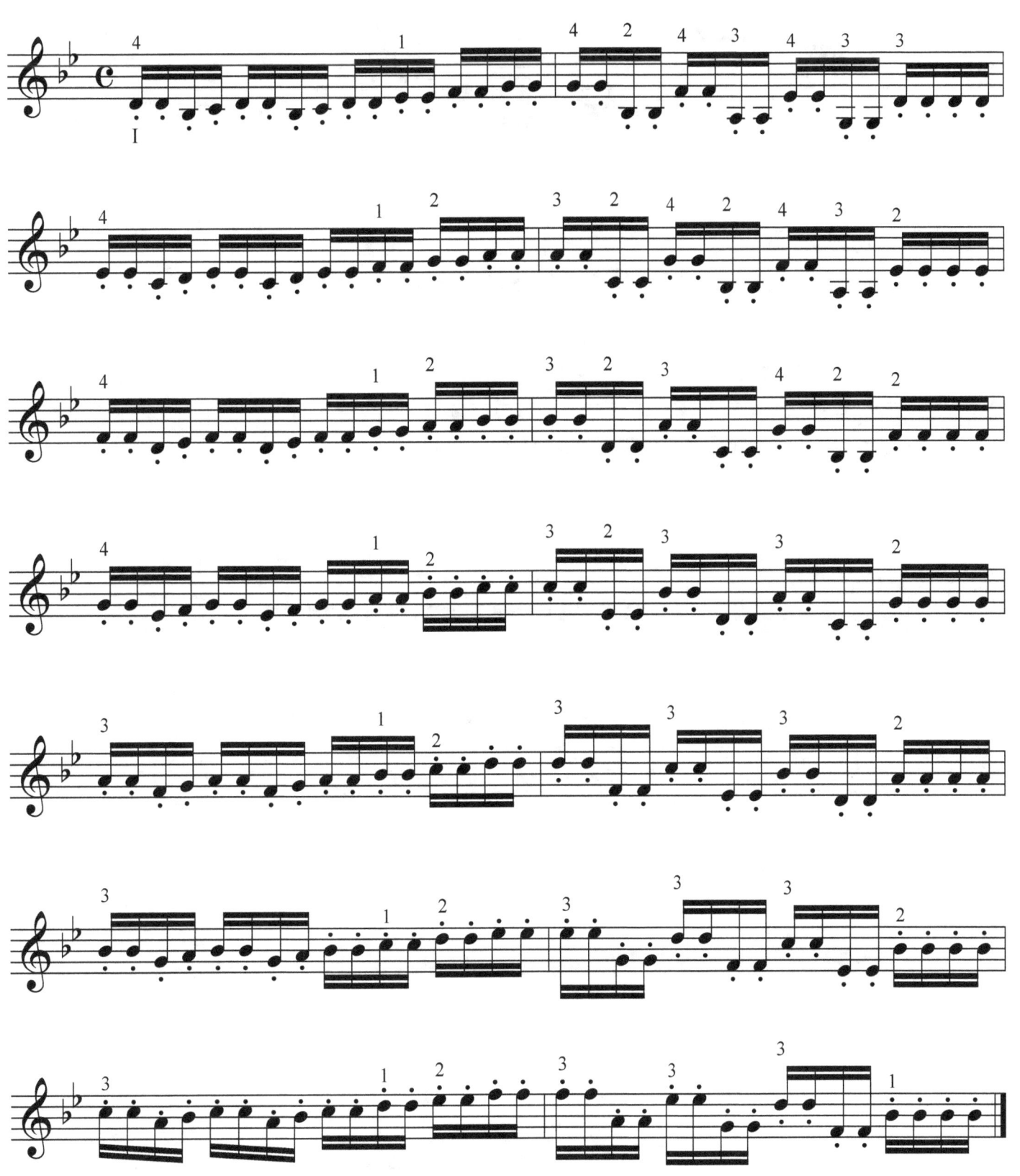

5

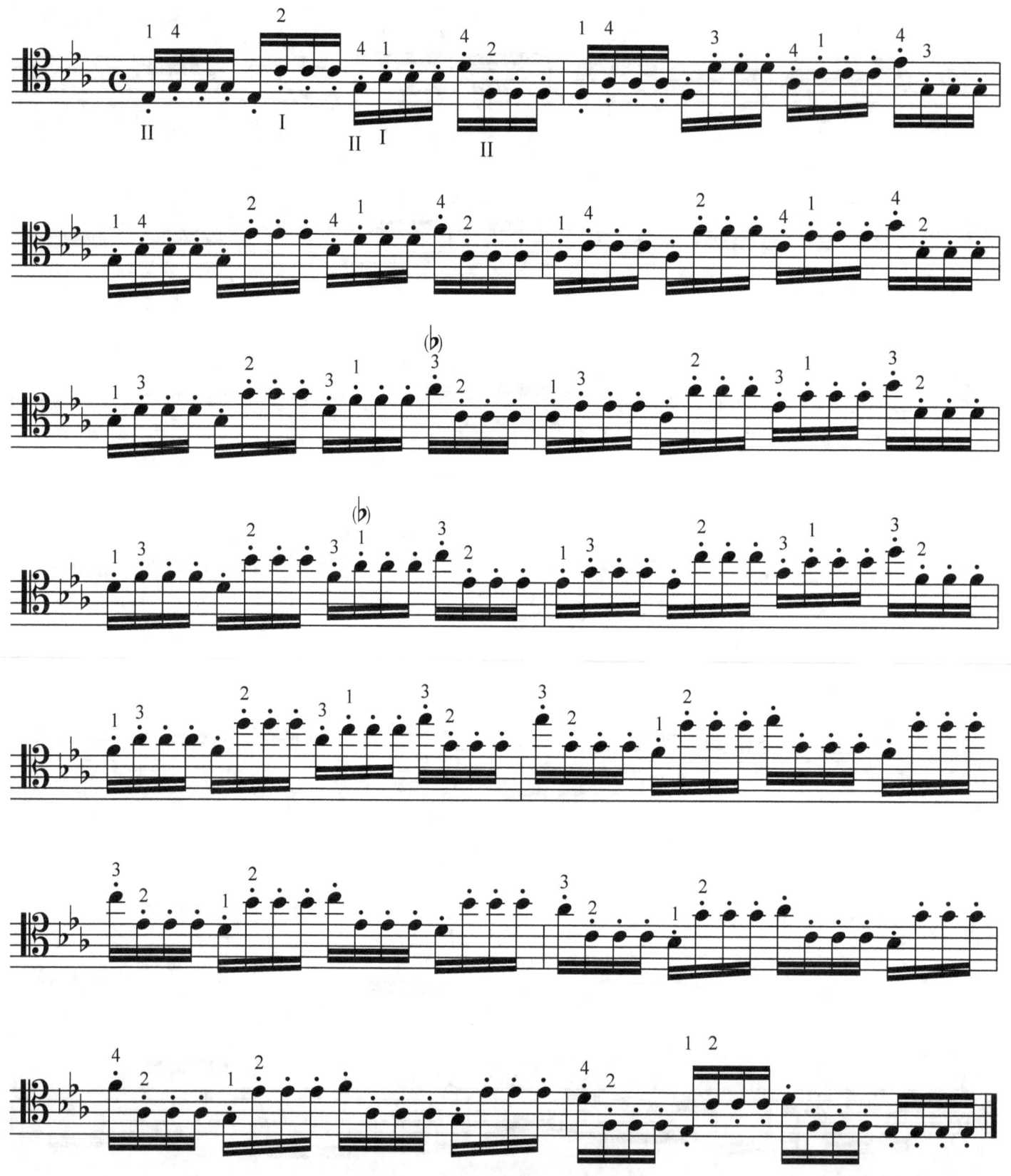

6

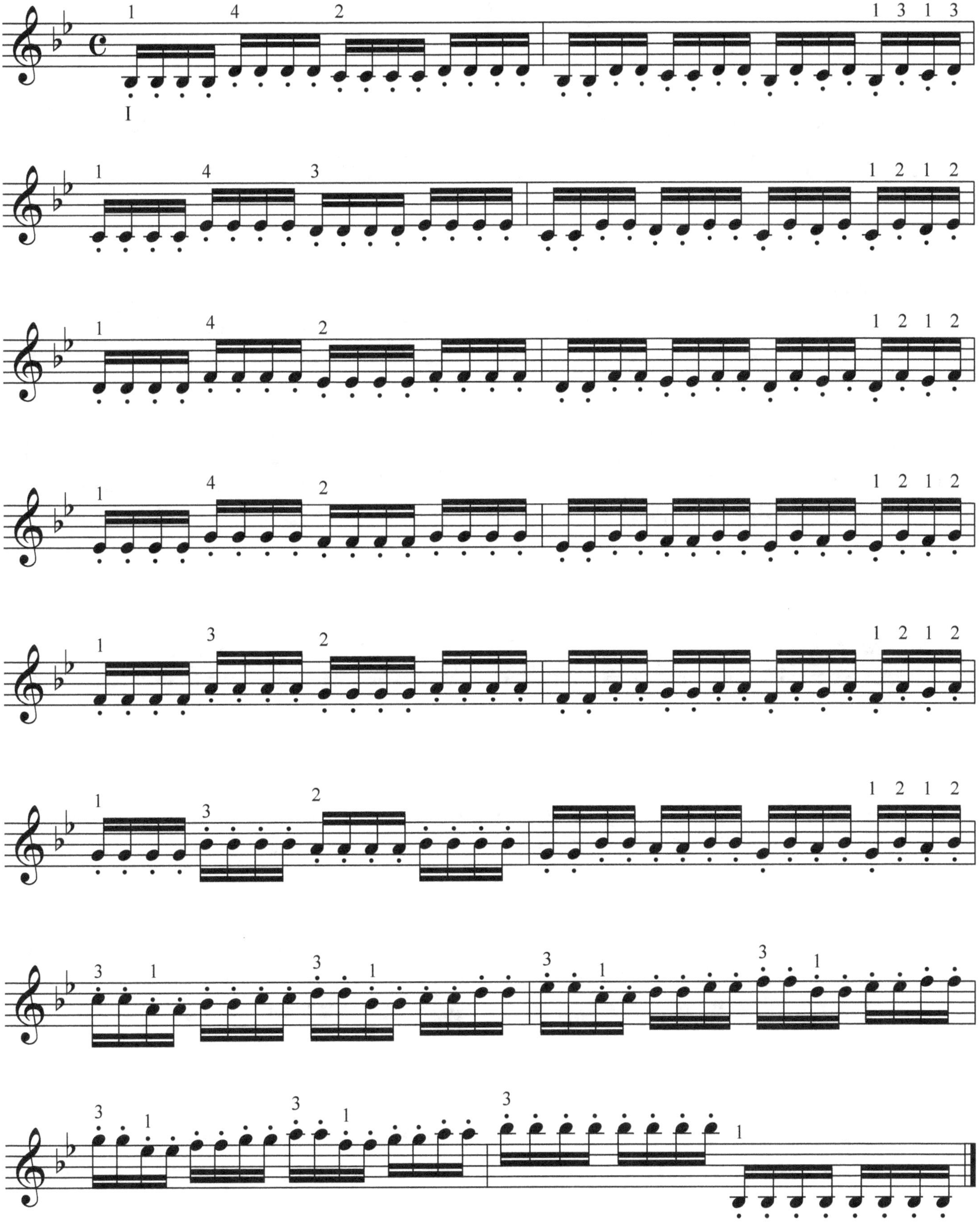

7

8

9

10

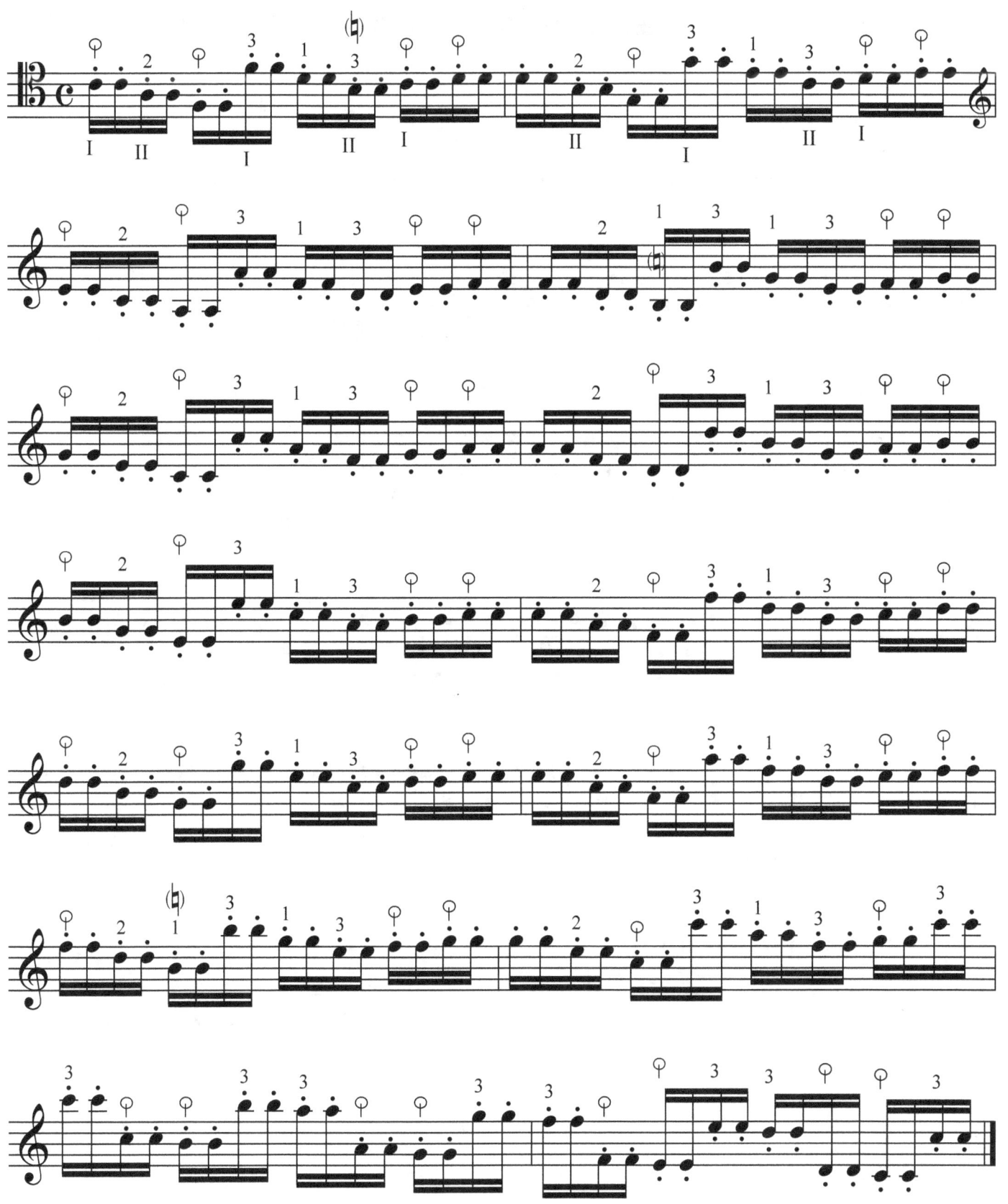

12

II

12

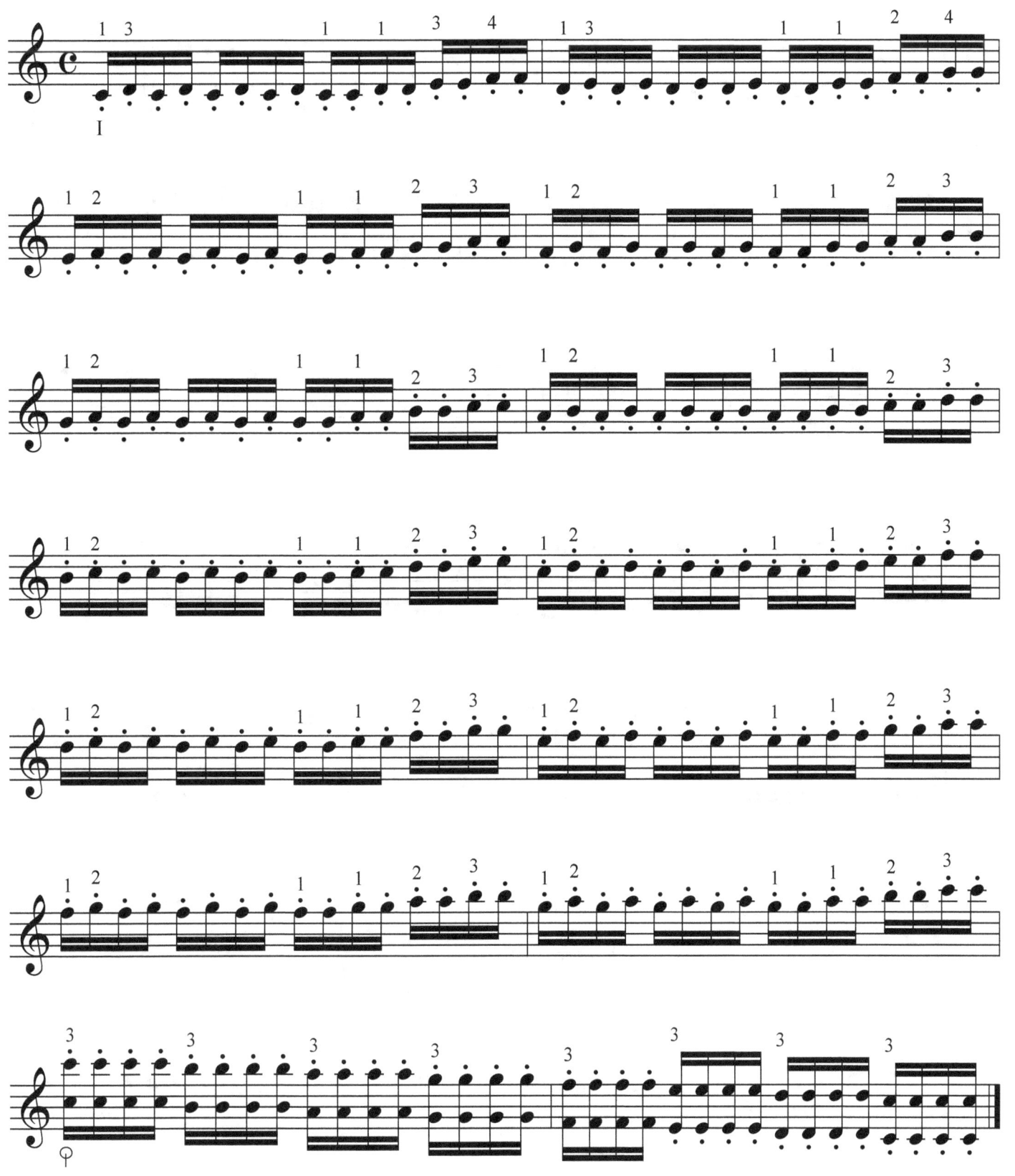

13

14

15

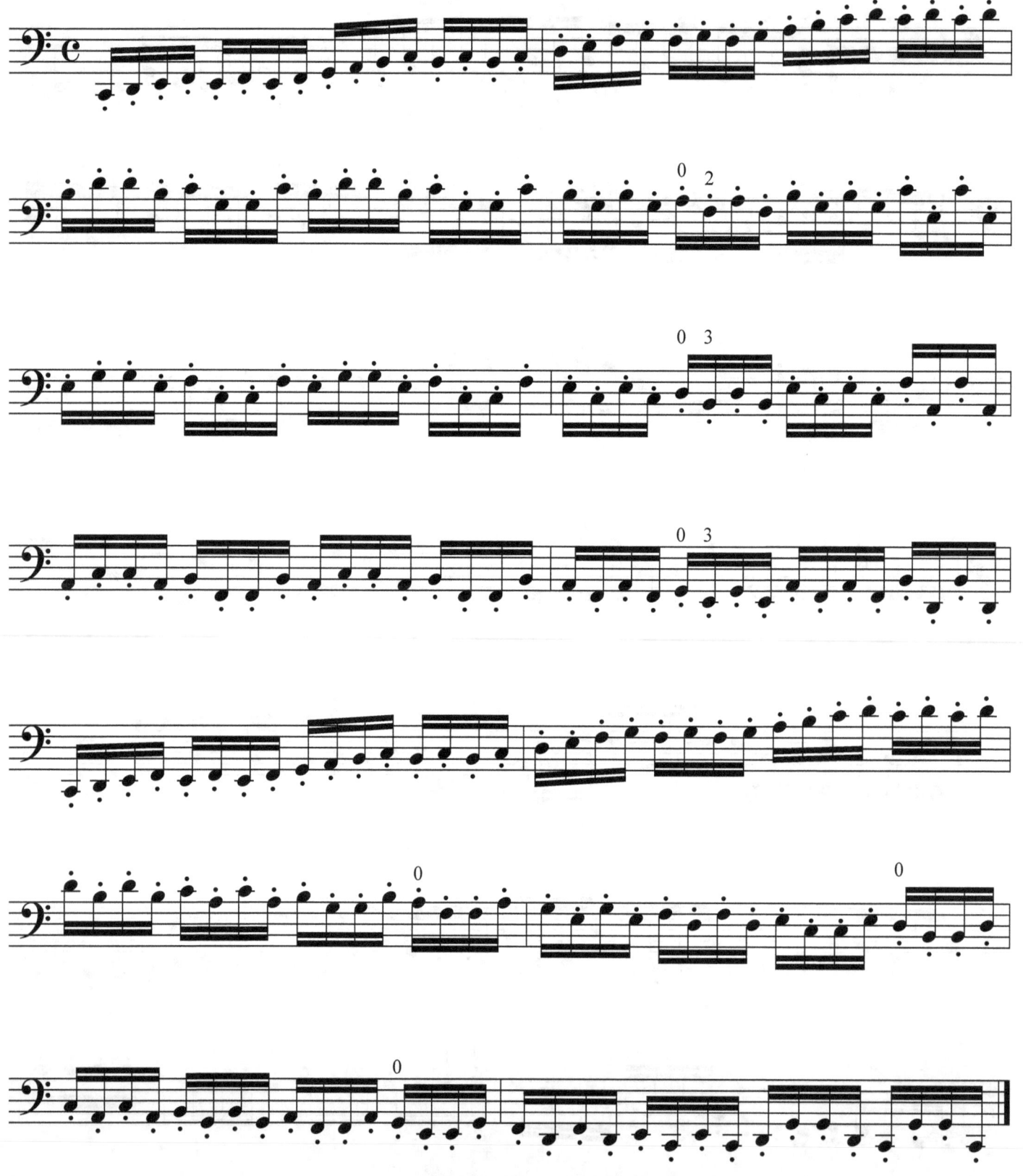

Sautille Studies for the Cello, Book One

16

©2006 C. Harvey Publications All Rights Reserved.

17

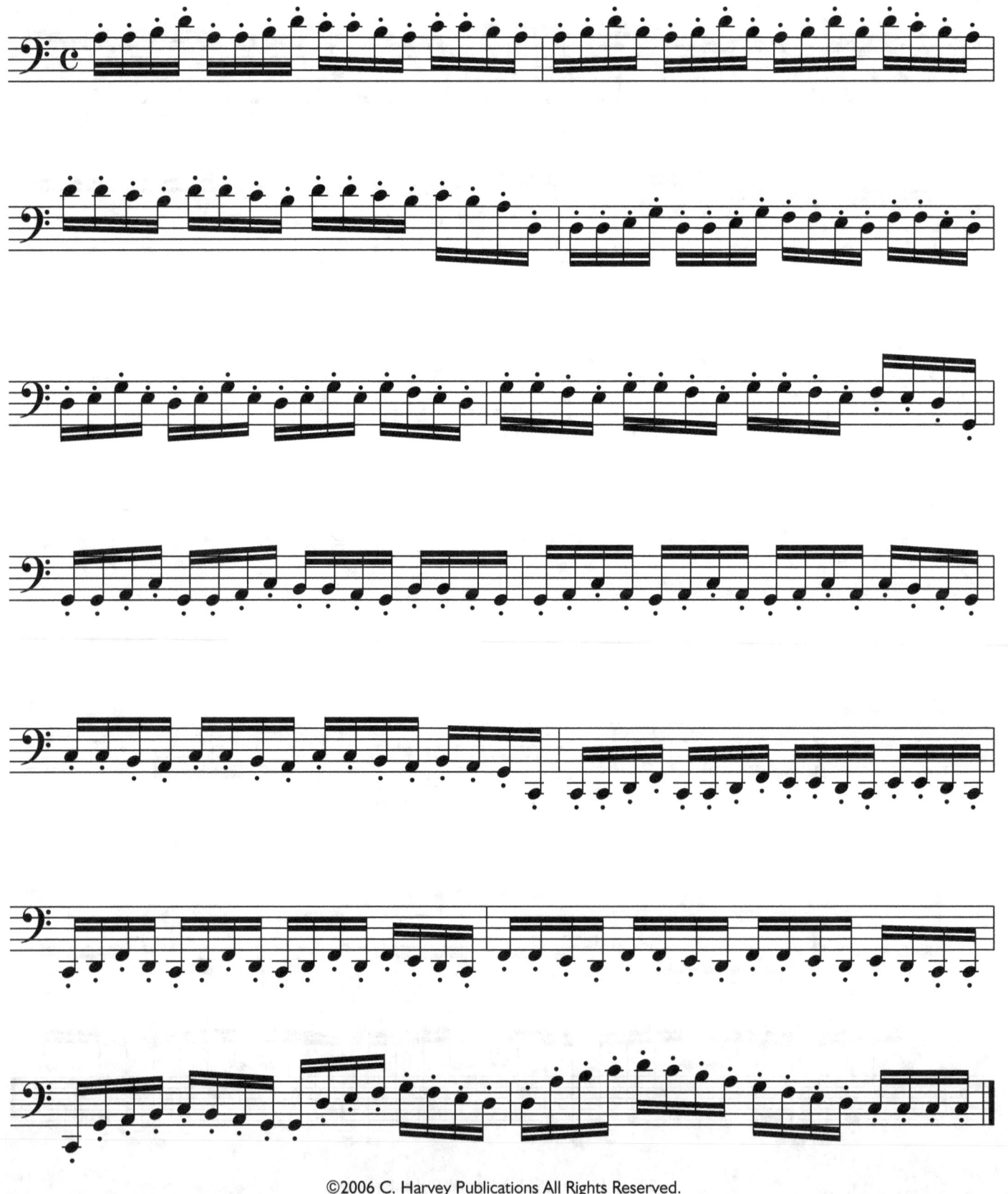

Sautille Studies for the Cello, Book One

18

19

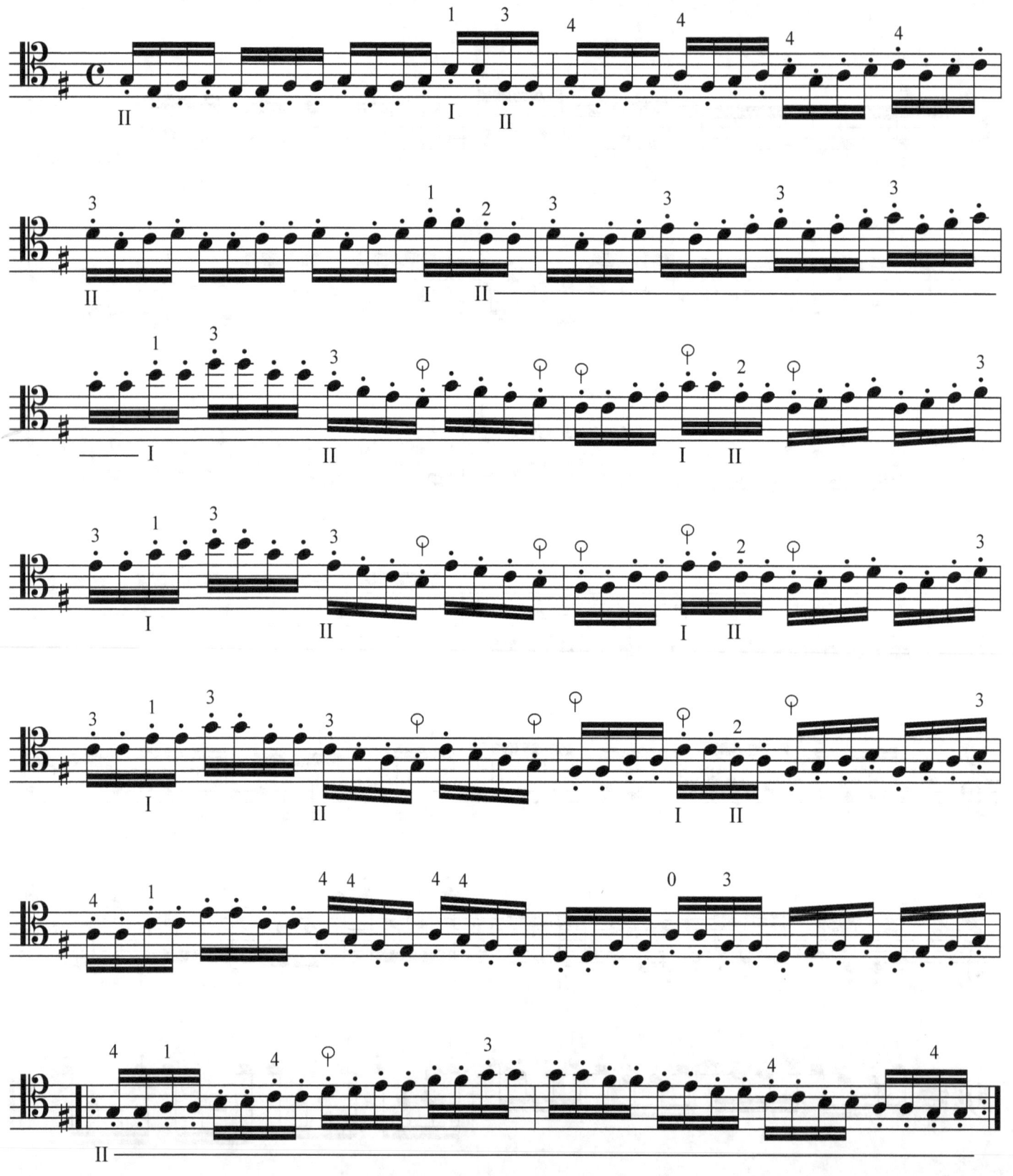

©2006 C. Harvey Publications All Rights Reserved.

Sautille Studies for the Cello, Book One

20

©2006 C. Harvey Publications All Rights Reserved.

21

Sautille Studies for the Cello, Book One

22

©2006 C. Harvey Publications All Rights Reserved.

23

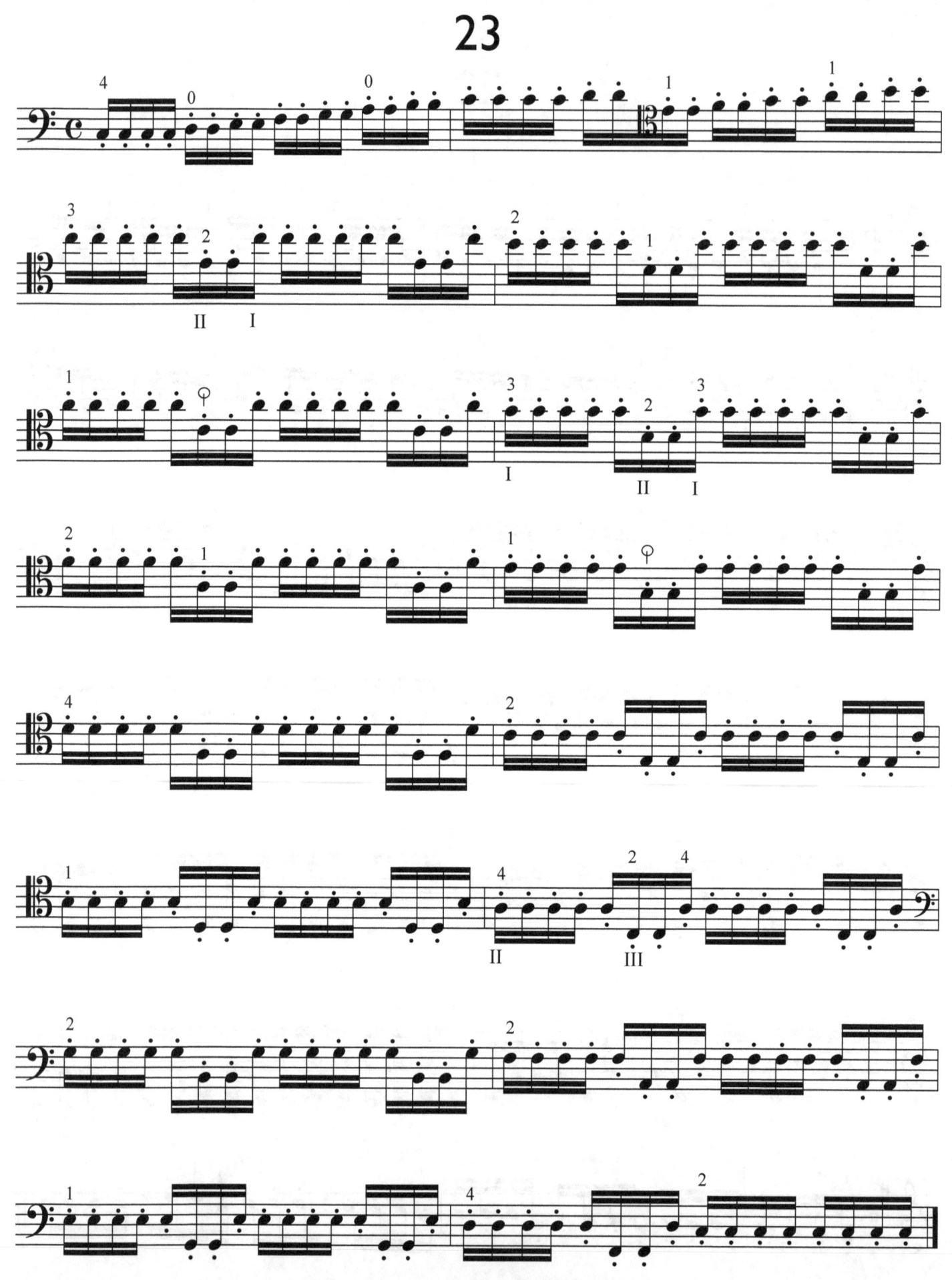

Sautille Studies for the Cello, Book One

©2006 C. Harvey Publications All Rights Reserved.

24

25

26

27

This entire page is played on the D string.

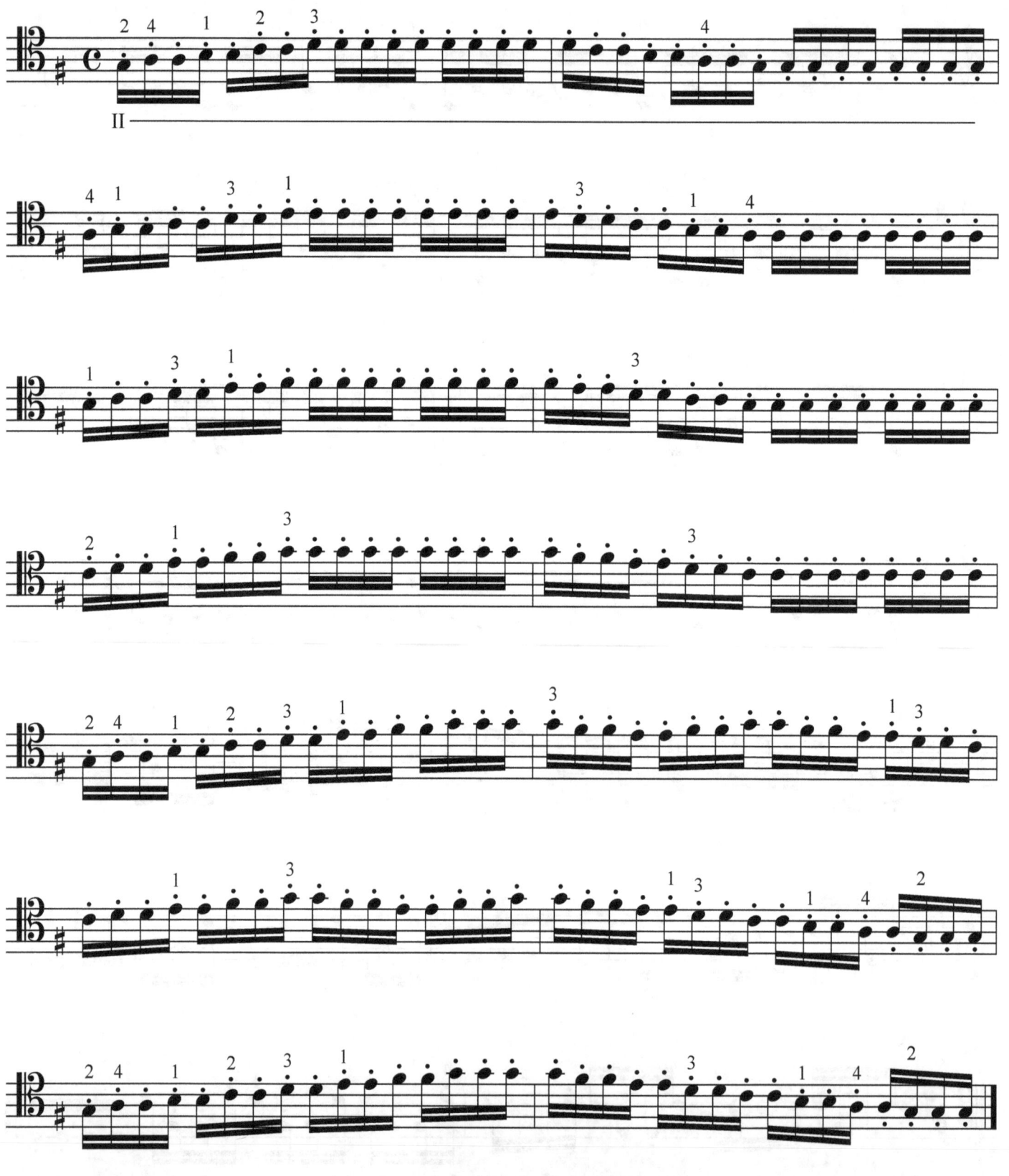

28

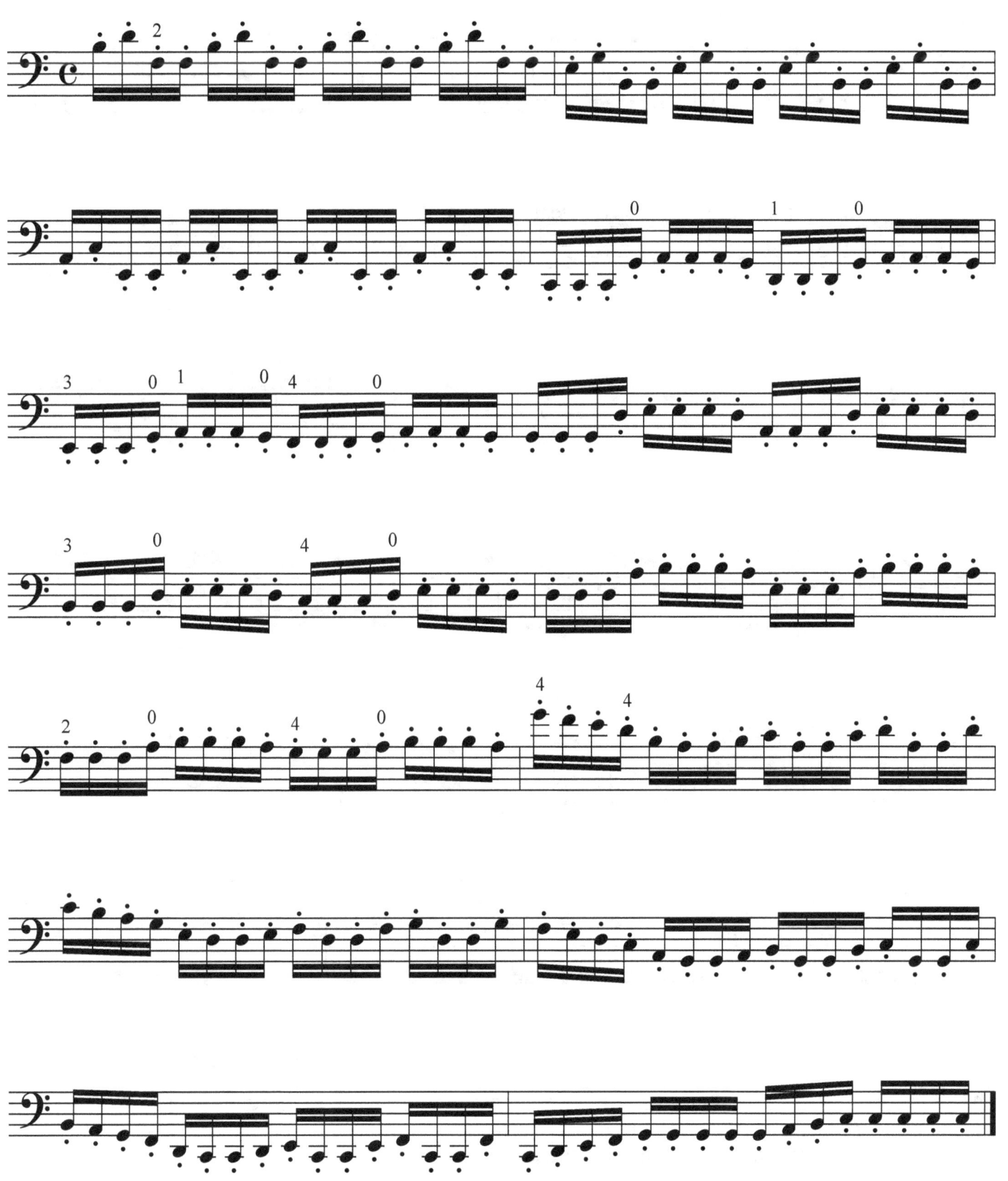

Sautille Studies for the Cello, Book One

30

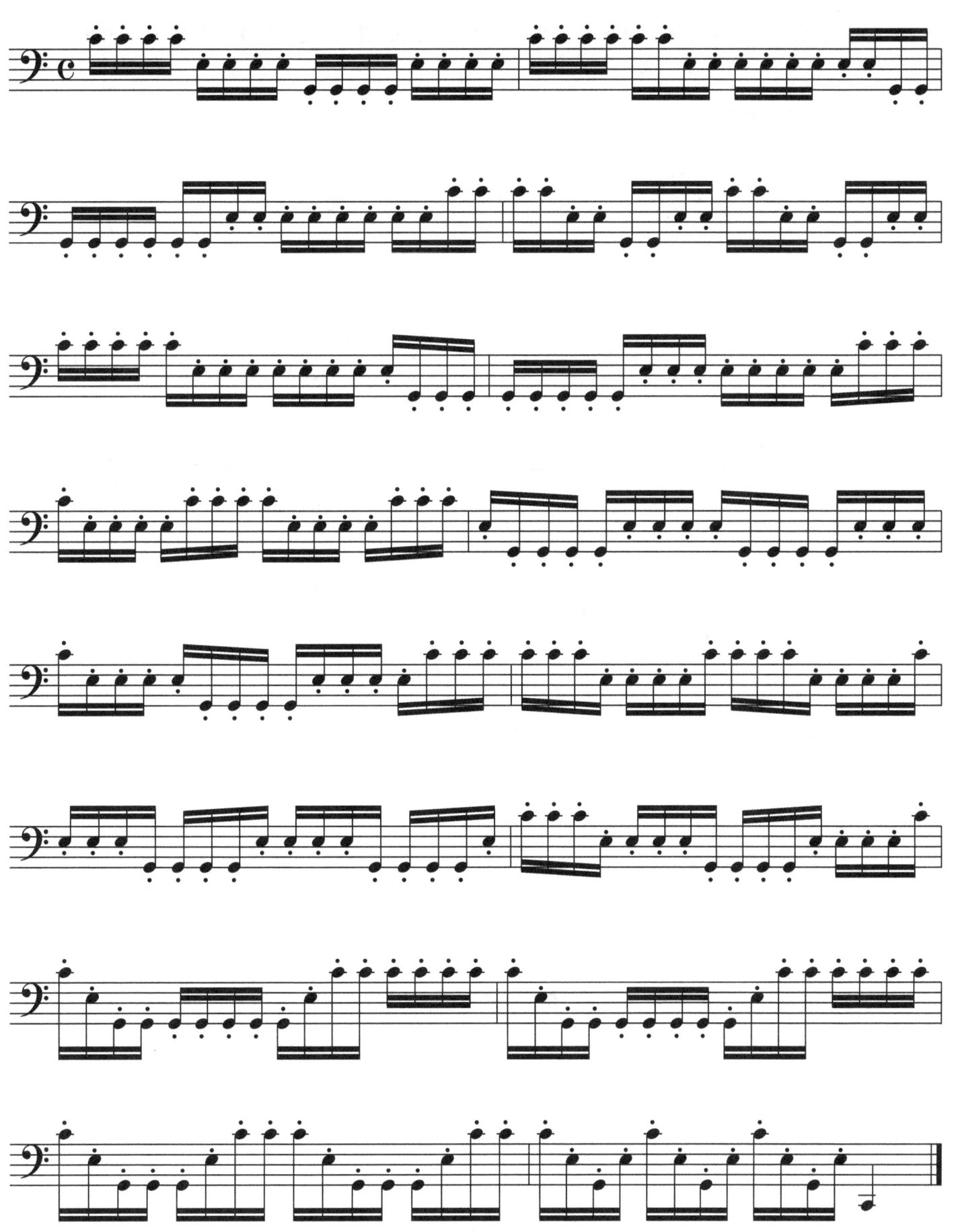

Bowing Studies on Arpeggios, for the Cello, Book One

1

String Crossing

Cassia Harvey